FLUTE

CONCERT FAVORITES

Volume 1

Band Arrangements Correlated with Essential Elements Band Method Book 1

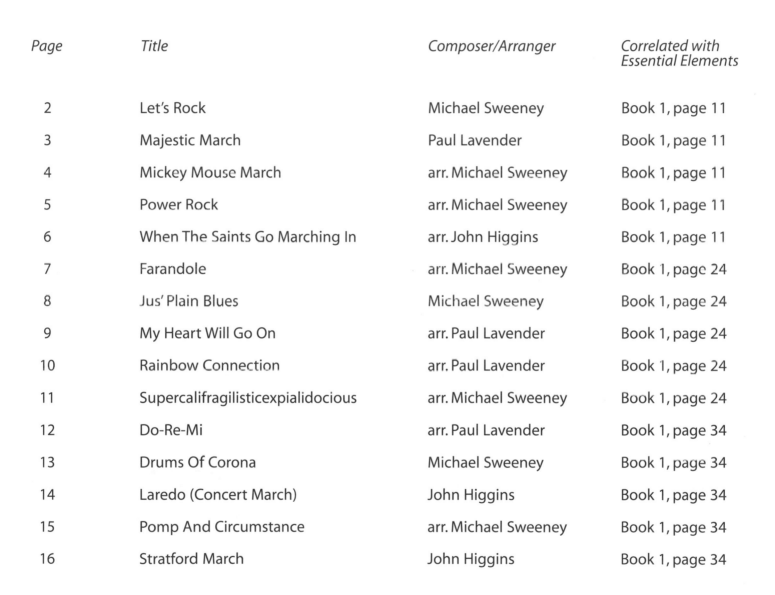

ISBN 978-0-634-05199-9

HAL•LEONARD®

7777 W. BLUEMOUND RD. P.O. BOX 13819 MILWAUKEE, WI 53213

00860119

LET'S ROCK!

FLUTE

MICHAEL SWEENEY (ASCAP)

MAJESTIC MARCH

FLUTE

By PAUL LAVENDER

00860119

MICKEY MOUSE MARCH
(From Walt Disney's "THE MICKEY MOUSE CLUB")

Flute

Words and Music by JIMMIE DODD
Arranged by MICHAEL SWEENEY

00860119

POWER ROCK

(We Will Rock You • Another One Bites The Dust)

FLUTE

Arranged by MICHAEL SWEENEY

WHEN THE SAINTS GO MARCHING IN

Words by KATHERINE E. PURVIS
Music by JAMES M. BLACK
Arranged by JOHN HIGGINS

FLUTE

FARANDOLE
(From "L'Arlésienne")

Flute

Georges Bizet
Arranged by MICHAEL SWEENEY (ASCAP)

00860119

JUS' PLAIN BLUES

FLUTE

MICHAEL SWEENEY (ASCAP)

From the Paramount and Twentieth Century Fox Motion Picture TITANIC

MY HEART WILL GO ON

(Love Theme From 'Titanic')

Music by JAMES HORNER
Lyric by WILL JENNINGS
Arranged by PAUL LAVENDER

Flute

Moderately

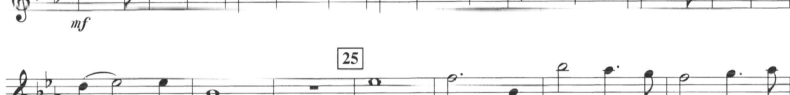

00860119

From THE MUPPET MOVIE

THE RAINBOW CONNECTION

Words and Music by PAUL WILLIAMS
and KENNITH L. ASCHER
Arranged by PAUL LAVENDER

Flute

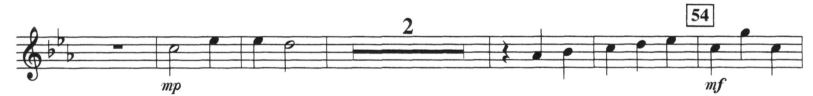

From Walt Disney's MARY POPPINS

SUPERCALIFRAGILISTICEXPIALIDOCIOUS

Words and Music by
RICHARD M. SHERMAN and **ROBERT B. SHERMAN**
Arranged by MICHAEL SWEENEY

FLUTE

Flute

DO-RE-MI

Lyrics by OSCAR HAMMERSTEIN II
Music by RICHARD RODGERS
Arranged by PAUL LAVENDER

00860119

DRUMS OF CORONA

FLUTE

MICHAEL SWEENEY (ASCAP)

LAREDO
(Concert March)

FLUTE

JOHN HIGGINS

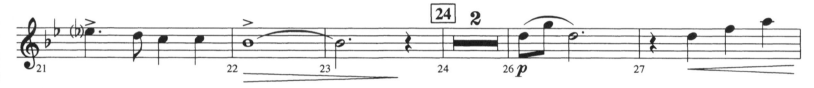

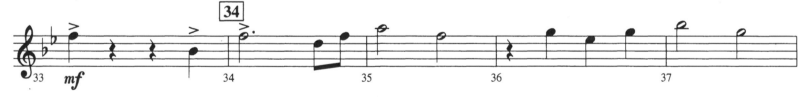

POMP AND CIRCUMSTANCE
March No. 1

Flute

By EDWARD ELGAR
Arranged by MICHAEL SWEENEY

5 *Play on repeat only*

13

21

3 *Play both times* **29**

37

1. Optional repeat to measure 5

2. Optional repeat to measure 29

3.

00860119

STRATFORD MARCH

FLUTE

JOHN HIGGINS (ASCAP)

00860119